W9-BUM-656

RECEIVED
MAY 0 2 2011
By _____

HAYNER PUBLIC LIBRARY DISTRICT
ALTON, ILLINOIS

OVERDUES .10 PER DAY, MAXIMUM FINE
COST OF ITEM
ADDITIONAL $5.00 SERVICE CHARGE APPLIED TO
LOST OR DAMAGED ITEMS

HAYNER PLD/ALTON SQUARE

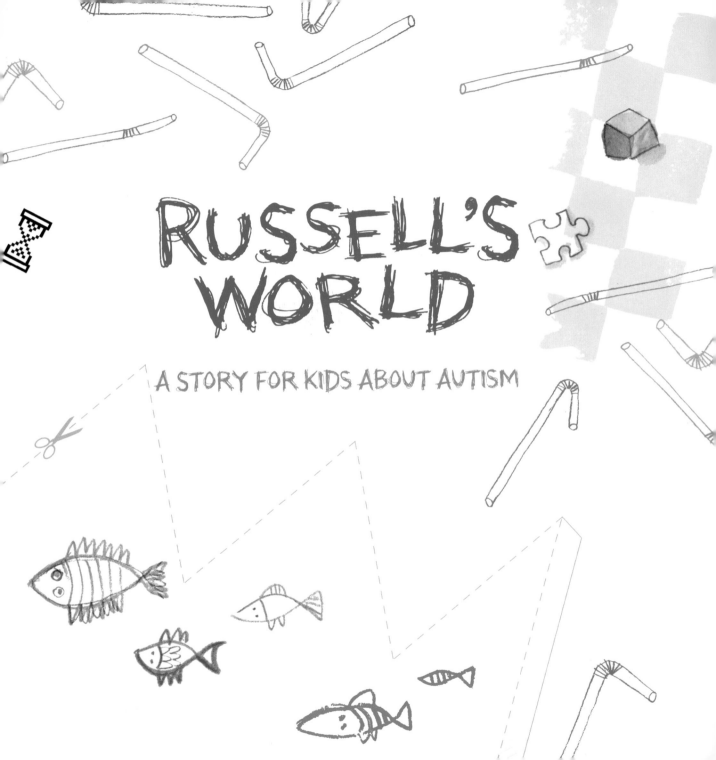

RUSSELL'S WORLD

A STORY FOR KIDS ABOUT AUTISM

Copyright © 2011 by Magination Press. All rights reserved.
Except as permitted under the United States Copyright Act of 1976, no part of this publication may be reproduced or distributed in any form or by any means, or stored in a database or retrieval system, without the prior written permission of the publisher.

Published by
MAGINATION PRESS
An Educational Publishing Foundation Book
American Psychological Association
750 First Street, NE
Washington, DC 20002

For more information about our books, including a complete catalog, please write to us, call 1-800-374-2721, or visit our website at www.maginationpress.com.

Original photographs by Charles A. Amenta III
Design and illustrations by Monika Pollak and Gdańskie Wydawnictwo Psychologiczne
Printed by Worzalla, Stevens Point, WI

The author wishes to acknowledge Marie Grass Amenta's contribution to *Russell's World* and her continued support of the book. She drew on her extensive experience leading parent support groups to provide essential material to the Note to Parents.

Library of Congress Cataloging-in-Publication Data
Amenta, Charles A. (Charles Anthony)
 Russell's world : a story for kids about autism / by Charles A. Amenta III ; illustrated by Monika Pollak.
    p. cm.
 Originally published as: Russell is extra special. New York : Magination Press, c1992.
  ISBN 978-1-4338-0975-0 (hardcover) -- ISBN 978-1-4338-0976-7 (pbk.) 1. Amenta, Russell--Mental health--Juvenile literature. 2. Autistic children--Juvenile literature. 3. Autism--Juvenile literature. I. Amenta, Charles A. (Charles Anthony) Russell is extra special. II. Title.
 RJ506.A9A63 2011
 618.92'85882--dc22
            2010048837

10 9 8 7 6 5 4 3 2 1

RUSSELL'S WORLD

A STORY FOR KIDS ABOUT AUTISM

BY CHARLES A. AMENTA III, MD
ILLUSTRATED BY MONIKA POLLAK

Magination Press • Washington, DC
American Psychological Association

618.92
AME

b19566517

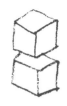

Russell is a kid with special differences. He has autism. This means his behaviors can be surprising in three big ways.

1. He likes to be alone. Other people don't seem to interest him as much as you might expect.
2. He can't talk, and it's hard for him to understand what people are saying.
3. He doesn't play the way other kids do.

Russell is nine. He has two younger brothers, Benjamin and Gregory. Benjamin and Gregory love Russell, and Russell loves them! They know he has autism, so they make extra sure that they help him when he wants their help and leave him alone when he doesn't. Sometimes they play together, and have lots of fun.

Gregory and Benjamin ask their dad why Russell has autism. Their dad is a doctor, but he doesn't know the answer. Nobody knows why some kids have autism, but scientists are trying to figure it out. They do think that most kids with autism were just born that way.

When they are babies, some children with autism do not
snuggle when their parents cuddle them. Russell did!
Maybe that's why Russell has such a nice smile now.
He still likes tickling and cuddling with his mom.

Gregory and Benjamin like to play with friends. Russell doesn't. He likes to be by himself. He goes far away or leaves the room when other kids come over.

All children with autism have difficulty making friends. As they get bigger, they usually become more OK being around other people.

Children with autism also have a hard time learning to talk. Russell can't talk at all. Some other kids repeat things like an echo. They may confuse "you" and "I." They say, "You want a cookie," when they mean "I want a cookie." Sometimes their voices sound flat and mechanical when they talk, like a robot or computer.

Russell hums, babbles, laughs, and screams. Russell screams when he's unhappy and when he's excited. Sometimes he laughs really loudly— and then he screams. It's not always easy to understand what Russell is feeling and why his mood changes so quickly.

Russell's parents and teachers teach him sign language. He knows signs for "eat," "drink," and "more." When Russell makes his sign for "more," it looks like he's praying or clapping.

Gregory and Benjamin think it's fun to use sign language, but Russell would rather hand someone his cup when he's thirsty. Sometimes he pulls his mom's hand and puts it on the refrigerator door to show her that he wants something to eat.

Russell loves to eat! His favorite foods are pizza and PB&J sandwiches. He likes to eat with his fingers, even when his parents want him to use a fork. When nobody is looking, he picks the toppings off the pizza and leaves the crust. He opens up his sandwich and smears his peanut butter. Russell's mom and dad are teaching him to be less messy!

When he was little, Russell started ignoring his mom and dad when they said his name. Sometimes Russell covers his eyes or pulls at his eyelids instead of looking at his family. To encourage Russell to pay attention more often, his parents give him a Cheerio every time he responds to them.

Giving Russell Cheerios might sound surprising to you. Benjamin and Gregory learn better by hearing proud encouragement or feeling a warm hug. But Russell likes to eat! A lot of children with autism learn best in surprising ways.

It's hard for Russell to learn things because his autism is severe. (Severe means really serious or bad or hard.) He can use the potty and get dressed by himself, but it took him a long time to learn.

Not all kids with autism have a hard time learning. Some are really smart and a few are even extraordinary! They can do things like multiplication without paper or a calculator. Others can play the piano well. Russell is like a detective because he can find things that are hidden——like straws and Cheerios. Even if they are smart or talented or good at finding things, kids with autism usually need extra, special help, especially to make friends.

Most kids learn by imitating (or copying) others. They learn while they play and use their imaginations. Benjamin and Gregory pretend to conduct music like their mom does. Gregory pretends he's a doctor like his dad. Benjamin pretends to take pictures of Russell with a toy camera.

Russell would rather put the toy camera in his mouth. Russell does not copy other people. Children with autism usually don't play pretend. They might not play like other kids. Sometimes they like to do things over and over and over again——like lining up toy cars but not making car sounds.

Some children with autism like to spin toys—even toys that are not made for spinning! Many like shiny things, like spoons or doorknobs.

 Russell has a special timer that he likes to stare at. Inside the timer, a bright green liquid flows from top to bottom.

Russell likes to carry a plastic straw wherever he goes. He folds it and pinches it between his thumb and fingers. He also likes to look out the window and tap on it with plastic toys. Sometimes he likes tapping with just his hands.

37

Russell goes to school. He really likes riding the bus. He's in a class with other kids who are like him because they need special help. The kids on the bus save Russell's favorite seat for him. He loves having the same seat every trip.

At school, he learns simple tasks and sign language. The teachers also help him with manners and playing with the other kids.

Russell *loves* swinging on the swing set at school. Kids like to rock back and forth to music and to whirl around, but kids with autism usually *love* to whirl and rock. It's sometimes their favorite way of playing.

Russell walks gracefully. He's learning to swim, and he *loves* the water. Not all children with autism are graceful. Some can be really clumsy, but not Russell!

Children with autism can be really sensitive and might get mad if something they like changes. They notice if their favorite toy is moved even a tiny bit. Russell wants everything to be on time, especially dinner.

Russell sometimes causes problems. He tears down wallpaper, eats toothpaste, and even breaks Gregory's and Benjamin's toys. That can make them very angry, but they love Russell and know that he's not being mean or bad. They're also good at finding other things to play with.

Nighttime is hard for Russell. Sometimes he wakes up and screams or cries or giggles. Sometimes he is too excited to stay in bed.

Sometimes, Russell has temper tantrums at night. When that happens, he kicks his shins with his heel. He doesn't seem to care about the pain. Benjamin and Gregory can give him a cup of water to help him calm down. Luckily, they're good at going right back to sleep if Russell wakes them.

Even though autism can be hard, Russell is a happy boy who loves his family, and his family loves him right back!

Now you know more about Russell's world. When you see other children with autism, you won't be so surprised by their different behaviors, and you can love them, too.

cut

NOTE TO PARENTS

Autism is a severe developmental disorder. Children with autism have significant problems with social interactions and communication and a very restricted set of activities and interests. Its cause is thought to involve multiple genetic factors. Environmental factors, such as infection or other problems prior to birth, may also contribute but to what extent is unknown. Autistic behaviors are generally apparent before age two; however, the diagnosis is often not made until age three or later when language deficits are obvious.

Children with autism do not form typical social or emotional relationships with parents, siblings, or peers. Parents may have difficulty comforting them. Some children have a great aversion to being kissed or hugged, while others may insist on hugs or tickling. Even the highest functioning adults with autism have problems understanding another person's point of view or reciprocating socially or emotionally with others.

Difficulties in communication can be numerous, too. The child with autism may have little or no ability to use symbols of any kind and often has a poor understanding of spoken words. Language delays or a lack of communication skills are common, as is difficulty in sustaining conversations. Children with autism might confuse pronouns, repeat or echo phrases heard in the past, or have a ritualistic use of language. Children with autism often lack typical or age-appropriate play skills or the ability to engage in "pretend play."

Children with autism also have unusual patterns of behavior—adherence to rules and routines, preoccupation with specific parts of an object, repetitive movements like spinning themselves or repeated activities such as leaf tearing, or attachment to unexpected items like drinking straws.

HOW TO FIND SERVICES AND TREATMENT

Specialists such as clinical psychologists, child psychiatrists, or pediatricians who specialize in autism can recommend appropriate treatment and education programs. Children with autism under the age of 5 have been shown to benefit greatly from early, intensive, comprehensive treatment programs such as applied behavior analysis, speech and language therapy, occupational therapy, and social skills training. Programs shown to be successful for children of any age with autism have a number of common elements: a focus on communication, attention, and social skills; a highly structured school environment with low student-to-teacher ratio; a predictable home, school, and therapy environment; and a high level of structured family involvement. When parents are more involved in the treatment process, children are more likely to generalize and maintain what they learn in school and in therapy.

HOW YOU CAN HELP

Parents can help their children in small but important ways, starting with general reassurance and support. It's important to work with siblings to explain ways their family is different and to provide one-on-one time to make sure they don't feel left out. Self-care is crucial; don't forget to seek support for yourself while you're advocating for your child. And remember that you are a wonderful, concerned parent, but not a speech pathologist, audiologist, developmental pediatrician, or child psychologist—it is important to consult these specialists as soon as concerns arise.

PRACTICE PERSON-FIRST INTERACTION. Every child with autism is a child first who happens to have more numerous and more severe challenges than most children. Model desirable behaviors for your child the way you would for a child without autism, and practice how you respond when your child acts in surprising ways. For example:

- Greetings tend to be rituals in everyday life, so they're a great starting point. Modeling handshakes or high fives as appropriate greetings will help kids with autism fit in.
- Be patient. Sometimes it takes children with autism a while to respond.
- Demonstrate. For children with autism, it may be better to show them what to do rather than make a big, spoken explanation.
- Back off at obvious signs of distress. Remember that kids with autism are not always able to filter out all the sounds, crowds, light patterns, echoes, itchy fabrics, and other distractions that you are able to ignore. Sometimes things are just overwhelming.
- Educate your friends and family about autism. If you see someone mocking or chastising a child with autism, help them realize that some behaviors caused by autism have to be accepted and are not willful "bad kid" disruptions.
- Try to have as normal a family life as possible and encourage your children to just be kids. There are many places in most communities for your child with autism to participate in typical activities of childhood, such as sport teams and the Boy and Girl Scouts.
- Kids with autism are kids first. Whenever possible, refer to your child as a "person with autism," not an "autistic person."

EXPLAIN DIFFERENCES. Along with other books, *Russell's World* is a good tool for explaining the differences and the challenges of autism to kids. Kids who do not have a sibling with autism will see similarities to their own families. Siblings of children with autism, especially, will see scenes from Russell's life and know they are not so different.

A good way to use the book is to ask kids what is alike and what is different in Russell's world compared to their own. Siblings of kids with autism may see Russell as similar to their sib, but will also see differences. Starting with what is similar will make it easier to speak about what is different. It is important to answer questions in an age appropriate way, yet not overwhelm them with too much information. It might be good to begin with "he is different."

MAKE TIME FOR ALL YOUR CHILDREN. Siblings are important members of the family and their needs should be considered when decisions are being made for their affected sibling. Time alone with one or both parents is important. They will be more understanding and not as frustrated with their sibling if they know they will get "their time." Any special interest should be encouraged as well. Programs such as Sib Shops and others like it are a good way to help them understand they are not alone.

BE WARY OF DANGEROUS FADS. Always speak to a psychologist or pediatrician before trying or forgoing medical treatment. Although you may find many alternative therapies that claim to help children with autism, there are no magic bullets. No medications specifically target the disorder, although some can be useful for managing seizures or hyperactivity that sometimes occur in children with autism. Some alternative therapies can be harmful to your child (chelation therapy, for example, which the FDA has deemed dangerous and illegal as a treatment for autism). Almost all are expensive and can distract the family from therapies that might help.

You are an excellent resource for helping your child. However, if you find that your child's disorder greatly interferes with daily activities or you have difficulty coping with your family's situation, consult with a child psychologist or developmental specialist for further guidance. Additional strategies or treatment programs may be warranted. Also consider finding a family or parent support group. Autism is an isolating disability and often parents are afraid to ask for support or help. The Autism Society of America is a great place to find local, community-based or online support groups. Again, should further questions or concerns arise, seek guidance and advice with a developmental psychologist or clinical therapist.

ABOUT RUSSELL AND HIS FAMILY

Charles A. Amenta III, MD, and Marie Grass Amenta are the parents of three boys — Gregory, Benjamin, and Russell.

Years have passed since Charles and Marie first shared their family's story in *Russell Is Extra Special*. Russell and his brothers are adults now. Russell runs a small envelope stuffing business and has a deep love of music. Benjamin is a pianist, who occasionally plays organ, harpsichord, and cello. Gregory is a mathematician/physicist and percussionist. Marie is a choral conductor and is Founder and Music Director of the Midwest Motet Society. Although not a musician, Charles is the President of the Board of the Illinois Philharmonic Orchestra, and is an ear, nose, and throat physician, now in practice for 19 years.

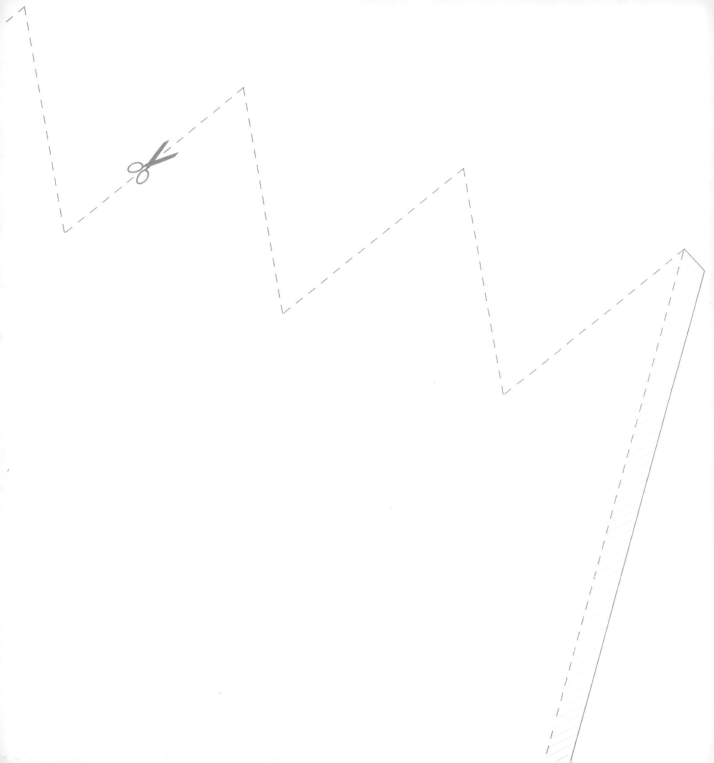